CHRISTIAN LEADERSHIP SERIES

Joy
in the
Parish

Hope
for
Pastor
and
People

Charles T. Knippel, Ph.D.

CPH
SAINT LOUIS

To Donna Marie,
My Beloved Wife and Partner in the Parish

Contents

Preface

For some time, after many years of pastoral and teaching ministry, I have wanted to write a book about the shape of the life together of pastors and people of God in Christian congregations. I have envisioned incorporating materials I have prepared for congregations, seminary courses, and a seminary continuing education course entitled "Pastoral Leadership: Factors in Personal Fulfillment and Parish Change." Because of certain events that have recently impacted my life, the task now seems more urgent to me. I will mention only a few of these events.

As will be noted again in the Introduction, at the turn of the millennium the Board for Higher Education of The Lutheran Church—Missouri Synod published a very informative and provocative study entitled the "Clergy Shortage Study." It revealed that today there are many joyless pastors and congregation members.

Recently I attended a voters assembly meeting of a small midwestern congregation. At that meeting an elder made a presentation on behalf of the Board of Elders in which he publicly and cruelly attacked and humiliated the pastor for not doing his job and for causing a variety of congregational woes, in particular the shrinking size of the congregation. The elder said he loved the pastor and desired only to speak the truth in love. But his affirmations were not supported by his manner, his tone of voice, and the content of his presentation. There was no joy for either pastor or people at that congregational meeting.

Also recently, when my wife and I were spending time at a lake not far from our home, the folks staying next to us came over for a short visit. It turned out that the husband and wife were members of a small Missouri Synod Lutheran congregation that they had helped organize. When they learned that I am a retired Missouri Synod pastor and seminary professor, they began to share thoughts and feelings about their current pastor and how unhappy they were with him because they experienced him to be controlling, disrespectful, and rigid in his dealings with people. In fact, they reported, they sometimes went to church about 20 miles from home because the pastor is friendly, warm, and evangelical. Once, when their pastor telephoned them on a Saturday evening to ask about their well-being, they told him they had been visiting a nearby congregation. He responded by instantly asking them if they would like to transfer their membership. What was going on? Where was the joy?

Could similar scenarios and stories of unhappiness be found throughout the church? There is evidence that such is the case. If so, we very much need to talk together about how to foster joy in the parish for both pastors and people. We follow the example of St. Paul who said, "We work with you for your joy" (2 Corinthians 1:24) and "We have the promise that joy is a gift of the Holy Spirit" (Galatians 5:22).

Introduction

The word is out that there is a lack of joy in many Christian parishes (congregations) for both pastors and people. As previously mentioned, a compelling witness to the reality of this joylessness are the findings of the "Clergy Shortage Study" prepared for the Board for Higher Education of The Lutheran Church—Missouri Synod and published at the turn of the millennium.

The purpose of this book is to increase joy in parishes, the joy of both pastors and parishioners. In keeping with this goal, I will review the nature and mission of the church and the roles of pastors and all God's people. I will discuss reasons for the lack of joy in Christian congregations for both pastors and people, and offer suggestions for increasing joy among the people of God as they live out their lives as members of a Christian community. Resources for this study are Holy Scripture, insights from family systems theory and church leadership principles, and contributions of health professionals.

Basic to my approach is the belief that to live joyfully in the Christian parish we need right understandings rooted in, and consistent with, the teachings of Holy Scripture and that are implemented among us by the working of the Holy Spirit by virtue of the saving work of Jesus Christ so carefully designed by God the Father. Thus this study very much focuses on understandings because how we understand influences how we believe, feel, and behave. If we have wrong understandings, we act in counterproductive ways. When we have correct understandings, we believe, feel, and act in ways that God approves and that benefit us and others. We will become more and more like the disciples in Antioch of Pisidia, mentioned by Luke in the Acts of the Apostles, who "were filled with joy and the Holy Spirit" (Acts 13:52).

This book is intended to provide helpful and hopeful words for pastors and people, especially for pastors and people in their life together. While it is crafted with careful attention to biblical and theological accuracy, it is written without dependence on professional theological jargon. I want this exploration to be useful to a broad variety of readers. May it be so by the goodness of God. Let there be joy in the parish!

Part: 1

Scriptural Words concerning the Joyful Mission and Ministry of the Church

1

Joy Is God's Gift to His People, the Church

The Church Is People: God's People

We talk about church in various ways. We refer to denominations as church. For example, we talk about The Lutheran Church—Missouri Synod. In turn, we speak of the local congregation of Christians, which may possibly include unbelievers on its membership role, and its worship facility as church. For example, we refer to The Lutheran Church of the Risen Christ, Trinity Lutheran Church, Zion Lutheran Church, and St. Paul Lutheran Church. However, when the New Testament uses the word *church*, it uses the term to designate people, the people of God gathered together at a particular location or locations or scattered throughout the world. In the Bible, then, the church is people, God's people. Thus, when we think of church, we are to think of people, those people called out of the world by God to be His very own people. In fact, in the Greek New Testament the word for church means "the called-out ones." God Himself gathers together the people who are His church. By nature people are not God's people. When we are born into the world, we are separated from God and His life. St. Paul describes us as dead in transgressions and sins and as objects of God's wrath. To the Ephesians St. Paul wrote:

> As for you, you were dead in your transgressions and sins, in which you used to live when you followed the ways of this world and of the ruler of the kingdom of the air, the spirit who is now at work in those who are disobedient. All of us also lived among them at one time, gratifying the cravings of our sinful nature and following its desires and thoughts. Like the rest, we were by nature objects of wrath. (Ephesians 2:1–3)

But God has changed our fallen and alienated status and situation. By the saving work of His Son, Jesus, God has made it possible for us and all people to be restored to both His loving presence and life-transforming power. Jesus lived a life completely obedient to God and suffered an innocent death on a cross as the God-appointed way of making good for our sinfulness and sin. Jesus, the Son of God made man, traded places with us and paid the debt of our sin before God. Thus through God's gift of faith in Jesus as Savior, we are able to trust in Jesus for deliverance from sin and through that faith receive deliverance from the guilt, punishment, and power of sin. St. Paul wrote to Titus, "Jesus Christ . . . gave himself for us to redeem us from all wickedness and purify for himself a people that are his very own, eager to do what is good" (Titus 2:13–14). To the Ephesians Paul wrote, "For it is by grace you have been saved, through faith—and this is not from yourselves, it is the gift of God—not by works, so that no one can boast. For we are God's workmanship, created in Christ Jesus to do good works, which God prepared in advance for us to do" (Ephesians 2:8–10). We gratefully affirm the words of Paul: "God made him [Jesus] to be sin for us, so that in him we might become the righteousness of God" (2 Corinthians 5:21).

God has His own way of savingly touching, and acting in, human lives. He uses the "stuff" of life on planet Earth to work in the lives of people. For example, on the basis of the rescuing work of His Son, Jesus, God makes people His very own through water, the water of Holy Baptism. St. Paul testifies, "When the kindness and love of God our Savior appeared, he saved us not because of righteous things we had done, but because of his mercy. He saved us through the washing of rebirth and renewal of the Holy Spirit, whom he poured on us generously through Jesus Christ our Savior, so that, having been justified by his grace, we might become heirs having the hope of eternal life" (Titus 3:4–7).

We and all who are baptized into Jesus Christ and believe in Him as Savior and Lord are most certainly God's people whom He calls His church. This church God also calls the body of Christ. For our right understanding, as well as the correct understanding of the Corinthian Christians, St. Paul wrote about the church as the Christian people gathered at Corinth and wherever they might be in the world. To the Corinthians Paul commented, "Paul, called to be an apostle of Jesus Christ by the will of God and our brother Sosthenes, to the church in Corinth, to those sanctified in Christ Jesus and called to be holy, together with all those everywhere who call on the name of our Lord Jesus Christ—their Lord and ours" (1 Corinthians 1:1–3).

Speaking of the church as Christ's body, St. Paul wrote to the Corinthians about Baptism as entry into the church, "The body is a unit, though it is made up of many parts; and though all its parts are many, they form one body. So it is with Christ. For we were all baptized by one Spirit into one body—whether Jews or Greeks, slave or free—and we were all given the one Spirit to drink" (1 Corinthians 12:12–13). To the Romans Paul commented, "Just as each of us has one body with many members, and these members do not all have the same function, so in Christ we who are many form one body, and each member belongs to all the others" (Romans 12:4–5).

To sum up: The New Testament teaches that the church exists and acts in the shape of congregations of God's people gathered at specific places who are spiritually enlivened by God through the Gospel in Word and Sacraments.

The basic confessional document of the Lutheran Church, the Augsburg Confession, sums up what Scripture teaches about the church. "The Christian church, properly speaking, is nothing else than the assembly of all believers and saints" (Article VIII).

God Intends for His People to Have the Joy He Gives

God wants His people in parishes everywhere to have joy and happiness. One of the fruits of faith the Holy Spirit gives is joy (Galatians 5:22). God wants us and all His people, wherever we live together, to be like the disciples in Pisidian Antioch who "were filled with joy and with the Holy Spirit" (Acts 13:52). Paul wanted the members of the Corinthian congregation to share his joy (2 Corinthians 2:3). To the Philippians Paul wrote, "Rejoice in the Lord always. I will say it again: Rejoice!" (Philippians 4:4).

In our life together in Christ we and all believers are to experience joy, the joy of being Christians and the joy of living the Christian life in togetherness. Certainly, there are times in our life together when our joy and each other's joy will be threatened. Because, as Christians, we are not only forgiven and being renewed but also still sinners, we sometimes disobey God and hurt and disappoint one another. But still there is joy—the joy of forgiving others and being forgiven by others and the joy of living together under the lordship of Christ and caring for one another as we are cared for by God and fellow members of the body of Christ.

St. Paul himself told the Christians in Philippi how to maintain joy in the face of anxious moments we experience in the Christian fellowship. After he encouraged joy, Paul wrote, "Let your gentleness be evident to all. The Lord is near. Do not be anxious about anything, but in everything, by prayer and petition, with thanksgiving, present your requests to God. And the peace of God, which transcends all understanding, will guard your hearts and your minds in Christ Jesus" (Philippians 4:5–7).

2

God Gives the Church
Joyful Mission and Purpose

God Calls His People to Worship Him

God gives His people joy—the joy of salvation and the joy of belonging to the Christian church. He also gives His people the joy that comes from carrying out His purposes for the church.

First and foremost God gives joy to His people by calling His people to worship Him and empowering His people for that worship. This worship of the gathered people of God honors God and bestows God's grace for life with God here and hereafter. In fact, the Sunday worship of God's people is the source of life for the Christian. It is the epitome of the entire Christian life, of all that our Christian lives are to be. It is the life of the Christian compressed into a weekly action of fellowship that, by its very nature, shapes and empowers the entire Christian life and mission.

By God's own design, worship stands at the heart and center of the church's life and mission. This is the way it was at the very beginning of the church. Luke writes of the members of the congregation in Jerusalem, "They devoted themselves to the apostles' teaching and to the fellowship, to the breaking of bread and to prayer" (Acts 2:42). Of the congregation in Troas, Luke wrote, "On the first day of the week we came together to break bread. Paul spoke to the people" (Acts 20:7). The writer to the Hebrews urged his Christian readers, "Let us not give up meeting together" (Hebrews 10:25). These New Testament passages tell us some specific things about worship. The worship of the church joyfully acknowledges and celebrates the presence of Jesus Christ and centers in and revolves around the Word and Sacraments because Jesus bids us to proclaim and hear His Word and to do with bread and wine what He has commanded.

As God's people we have persuasive and compelling reasons to gather together for worship. First of all, we gather to worship because worship is both God-mandated and the natural God-designed response of the people of God to the goodness of God in Jesus Christ. We respond to God's grace as did the early Christians in Jerusalem. These Christians were drawn by the Spirit of God to worship God around Word and Sacrament.

Because we are the people of God, we worship to receive the Divine Service, that is, to receive from God Himself a rich supply of His love and life through Word and Sacrament. Like the people of God in every generation, we crave the pure spiritual milk of God's Word because by it we grow up in our salvation (1 Peter 2:2). We celebrate and receive the Lord's Supper because in this Holy Meal we share together in the body and blood of Christ and participate in the benefits of His sacrifice for us on the altar of the cross (1 Corinthians 10:14–21).

In response to God's grace, we honor God and offer the sacrifice of praise and thanksgiving. We use worship as a singularly important opportunity to do together what St. Peter and the writer to the Hebrews instructed.

St. Peter wrote, "As you come to him, the living Stone—rejected by men but chosen by God and precious to him—you also, like living stones, are built into a spiritual house to be a holy priesthood, offering spiritual sacrifices acceptable to God through Jesus Christ" (1 Peter 2:4–5). Similarly, the writer to the Hebrew Christians exhorted, "Through Jesus, therefore, let us continually offer to God a sacrifice of praise—the fruit of lips that confess his name" (Hebrews 13:15).

Worship provides us with a singular occasion to rededicate ourselves to God, to offer ourselves to God as living sacrifices. This is the kind of dedication St. Paul directs in Romans 12: "Therefore, I urge you, brothers, in view of God's mercy, to offer your bodies as living sacrifices, holy and pleasing to God—this is your spiritual act of worship" (Romans 12:1).

Like God's people throughout the ages, we use our worship services to nurture one another's faith and life in Christ. We share God's Word and the Holy Supper with one another. We sing the Word of God into the hearing of one another. As the Word is read and proclaimed, we speak it to one another. At the Lord's Table we share together the body and blood of Christ. St. Paul had this kind of mutual nurturing in mind when he wrote, "Let the word of Christ dwell in you richly as you teach and admonish one another with all wisdom, and as you sing psalms, hymns and spiritual songs with gratitude in your hearts to God" (Colossians 3:16). The writer to the Hebrews had this to say about the nurturing task of Christians at worship: "Let us consider how we may spur one another on toward love and good deeds. Let us not give up meeting together, as some are in the habit of doing, but let us encourage one another—and all the more as you see the Day approaching" (Hebrews 10:24–25).

Finally, in worship we, and all God's people, pray for all sorts and conditions of people. We do what St. Paul taught the young pastor Timothy to do. He wrote, "I urge, then, first of all, that requests, prayers, intercession and thanksgiving be made for everyone—for kings and all those in authority, that we may live peaceful and quiet lives in all godliness and holiness. This is good, and pleases God our Savior, who wants all men to be saved and to come to a knowledge of the truth" (1 Timothy 2:1–4). We remember that the early Christians earnestly devoted themselves to prayer (Acts 2:42).

When we consider the meaning of the worship of God's people around Word and Sacrament, we understand more clearly why God has designed worship and moved His people to worship and why worship stands at the heart and center of the church's life and mission. As we worship together and in our worship celebrate the presence of the Lord Jesus, we receive rich supplies of God's love and power for life. In response to His goodness, we honor God and offer to Him the sacrifice of ourselves and of prayer, praise, and thanksgiving. From our Sunday worship service we go into the world to live daily lives that worship and honor God and that express all that our corporate worship embodies, epitomizes, and empowers. We live the lives directed and empowered by our Lord's Day worship. Then, on the next Lord's Day we return to worship together and receive new direction and empowerment for another week of worshipful Christian living.

God Calls His People to Minister to One Another

As each of us nurtures one another's Christian faith and life in our worship together, so God calls us to minister day by day to one another as members together of the church, Christ's body. Throughout our lives we are to promote each other's spiritual growth and the building up of the whole church of God. In his Letter to the Ephesians the apostle Paul speaks eloquently of our calling to do works of service for the building up of the body of Christ. For growth into being more and more like Christ, we are to speak the truth in love to one another. We are to speak the truth without sacrificing either truth or love. Paul has this to say:

> It was he [Christ] who gave some to be apostles, some to be prophets, some to be evangelists, and some to be pastors and teachers, to prepare God's people for works of service, so that the body of Christ may be built up until we all reach unity in the faith and in the knowledge of the Son of God and become mature, attaining to the whole measure of the fullness of Christ. . . . Speaking the truth in love, we will in all things grow up into him who is the Head, that is, Christ. (Ephesians 4:11–13, 15)

In providing mutual care, we are concerned not only for one another's spiritual well-being but are also called to provide holistic care for one another. We are to care for one another physically and emotionally. St. Paul said, "As we have opportunity, let us do good to all people, especially to those who belong to the family of believers" (Galatians 6:10). Jesus teaches us the importance of feeding the hungry, giving drink to the thirsty, being hospitable to the homeless, giving clothes to those who have none, looking after the sick, and visiting the imprisoned. Jesus says that when we do these works of kindness, we are doing them to Him (Matthew 25:34–40). St. James asks what good it is to wish that a person keeps warm and is well fed, if we do nothing to meet that person's physical needs. He observes that "faith by itself, if it is not accompanied by action, is dead" (James 2:14–17). We recall that the early Christians had everything in common. "Selling their possessions and goods, they gave to anyone as he had need" (Acts 2:44–45).

In our ministry to one another we never want to omit spiritual care, but spiritual care is always to be accompanied by ministry for every human need. We never want to omit spiritual care. We have done nothing of great and eternal importance for people if we care only for their bodies, minds, and environments. After all, as persons we are essentially spiritual persons endowed by God with bodies and minds and a place to live on His good earth.

God Calls His People to Minister to the World

God commissions us and all people of His church to minister not only to one another, but to the world. In worship we witness to the presence and power of Jesus Christ to the world, and worship prepares us to minister to the world as the very presence of Jesus.

In ministering to the world, we are first to make disciples of people for Jesus Christ and win them for life in the body of Christ. We have the mandate of the Lord Jesus Himself. Matthew records the words of Jesus to His disciples, "All authority in heaven and on earth has been given to me. Therefore go and make disciples of all nations, baptizing them in the name of the Father and of the Son and of the Holy Spirit, and teaching them to obey everything I have commanded you" (Matthew 28:18–20). Luke tells us that Jesus said, "Repentance and forgiveness of sins will be preached in his name to all nations" (Luke 24:47).

Jesus preached the good news of the kingdom. As He preached, He also healed every disease and sickness. Since he has sent us to do what the Father sent Him to do (John 20:21), we, too, are to provide holistic care for the people of the world just as we do for the people of the church. While we always give priority to caring for people's spiritual needs, we do not neglect to care for their physical needs. Often only when we minister to people's physical needs do they trust us to care for them spiritually. But whether or not they hear and believe the good news of Jesus, we still look after the sick, feed the hungry, give drink to the thirsty, visit those in prison, and clothe those who need clothing. We are to be Christ to all people. "Jesus went through all the towns and villages, teaching in their synagogues, preaching the good news of the kingdom and healing every disease and sickness" (Matthew 9:35). "When he [Jesus] saw the crowds, he had compassion on them, because they were harassed and helpless, like sheep without a shepherd. Then he said to his disciples, 'The harvest is plentiful but the workers are few. Ask the Lord of the harvest, therefore, to send out workers into his harvest field' " (Matthew 9:36–38).

For the Fulfillment of Their Mission God Gives His People Spirit-Endowed Functions and Gifts

To make it possible for us to fulfill our mission, God has given us, and every one of His people, Spirit-endowed functions and gifts. St. Paul discusses this endowment of God in his first Letter to the Corinthians: "There are different kinds of gifts, but the same Spirit. There are different kinds of service, but the same Lord. There are different kinds of working, but the same God works all of them in all men. Now to each one the manifestation of the Spirit is given for the common good" (1 Corinthians 12:4–7).

In his Letter to the Romans Paul also speaks of the gifts of God for ministry and encourages us all to identify our gifts and use our gifts faithfully in fulfilling the mission of the church.

Just as each of us has one body and many members, and these members do not all have the same function, so in Christ we who are many form one body, and each member belongs to all the others. We have different gifts, according to the grace given us. If a man's gift is prophesying, let him use it in proportion to his faith. If it is serving, let him serve; if it is teaching, let him teach; if it is encouraging, let him encourage; if it is contributing to the needs of others, let him give gener-

ously; if it is leadership, let him govern diligently;
if it is showing mercy, let him do it cheerfully.
(Romans 12:4–8)

We have received a mission that calls for dedication
and a willingness to minister to people of the church
and world with energy and unselfishness. How good it is
to know that God outfits us with gifts for the work He
has given us to do! As St. Paul writes, "It is God who
works in you to will and to act according to his good
purpose" (Philippians 2:13).

3

God Equips His People for Mission

Worship Equips for Mutual Care

God equips His people for mission by the very way He designs the mission of His people and interrelates its components: worship, mutual care, and outreach.

As we have observed, the worship of the church facilitates the care people of the church have for one another. Mutual care takes place in the worship services of the people of God. We share Word and Sacrament with one another to strengthen each other's faith and life in Jesus Christ. We bring gifts for the purpose of providing spiritual and physical care for one another and others. At the same time, this mutual care that takes place in worship equips us to care for one another after we leave worship and go about our respective callings. In our daily lives we live out the care begun in worship and enabled by worship.

The example of the early Jerusalem Christians demonstrates that worship equips for mutual care among Christians as they go forth from worship and live day by day. Remember how Luke observes that the first Christians "had everything in common" and gave to "anyone as he had need" only after he notes that "they devoted themselves to the apostles' teaching and to the fellowship, to the breaking of bread and to prayer" (Acts 2:42–45). Luke, the author of Acts, affirms that the worship of the church facilitates and enables the care people of the church have for one another.

Worship Empowers Ministry to People in the World

Just as worship outfits people for mutual care, so worship also empowers people for outreach. In our celebration of the Holy Communion we begin to minister to the world. In our worship we bring gifts not only for the good of those of the household of faith but so that we may also do good for all people. In our worship, as St. Paul writes, we "proclaim the Lord's death until he comes" (1 Corinthians 11:26). We proclaim it not only to one another but also to people outside of the church who take note of our worship. They see us go into the Lord's house and know something of what we do there—that we sing hymns, pray, hear God's Word, and celebrate the Lord's Supper. They observe that we celebrate the presence of the living Jesus Christ.

Empowered by worship, we go forth to continue what we have begun—to be Christlike to the people and win them for Christ and His church.

Like Worship, Mutual Care in Our Daily Lives Outfits Our Ministry for All People

Begun in worship and continued in daily life, mutual care among the people of God, like worship itself, outfits Christians to minister to people of the world in the name and place of Jesus Christ. Applicable here are the words of St. Paul to the Galatians, "As we have opportunity, let us do good to all people, especially to those who belong to the family of believers" (Galatians 6:10). St. Paul is saying that as we learn how do to good to each other we become more proficient in doing good to people in all walks of life. As we care for one another, we become better equipped to care for people who are still outside the family of God.

Worship Signifies and Produces the Life of Worship

We gladly affirm that God provides us and all His people with the ability to carry out the Christian mission. We have observed that God does this by the way He relates the tasks of the church to one another, beginning with the actions of worship which in themselves provide the paradigm for the Christian life. As we gather together for worship in the name of Jesus and to celebrate His presence, we receive God's grace and praise Him, we care for one another, and we witness to the world. This is the way we live every day. Empowered by our worship together as God's people and all that goes on there, we seek every day to worship God with our lives, to look to God for love and life, to care for one another, and to minister to people who are not yet members of Christ's church. To be sure, God gives joy to His people by giving us both a joyful mission and the ability to carry it out.

4

God Provides Pastors for His People

God Gives Pastors to His Church Gifts of His Goodness

God, who calls people into the Church and gives them a mission to carry forward, provides pastors for the benefit of His people. God Himself has instituted the pastoral ministry as a source of joy for His people. When the risen Christ appeared to His disciples, He said to them, " 'As the Father has sent me, I am sending you.' And with that he breathed on them and said, 'Receive the Holy Spirit. If you forgive anyone his sins, they are forgiven; if you do not forgive them, they are not forgiven' " (John 20:21–23). Jesus sent His disciples, filled with the Holy Spirit, to minister the Law and Gospel for the well-being of people, especially to proclaim the Gospel for the joy and edification of His holy people.

In his address to the elders of the church at Ephesus St. Paul spoke of them as men made overseers by the Holy Spirit to shepherd God's people (Acts 20:28). In his Letter to the Ephesians, Paul taught his readers that pastors, together with apostles, prophets, and evangelists, are gifts of Christ to His church (Ephesians 4:9–13). To Titus Paul wrote that things are unfinished in the church until elders are appointed. He wrote, "The reason I left you [Titus] in Crete was that you might straighten out what was left unfinished and appoint elders in every town, as I directed you" (Titus 1:5). Clearly, at least in some situations, the whole church at a particular place joined the apostles and elders in choosing men for pastoral ministry. This was the case in Jerusalem. "The apostles and elders, with the whole church, decided to choose some of their own men and send them to Antioch with Paul and Barnabas. They chose Judas (called Barsabbas) and Silas, who were leaders among the brothers" (Acts 15:22).

God Calls Pastors to Minister to His People

God calls certain men to carry forward a ministry for the joy and effectiveness of His people in carrying out their mission. God calls them to minister to His people as their elders, overseers, and shepherds (pastors), who care for and serve them with, and according to, the Word of God. St. Peter had this to say, "To the elders among you, I appeal as a fellow elder, a witness of Christ's sufferings and one who also will share in the glory to be revealed: Be shepherds of God's flock that is under your care, serving as overseers" (1 Peter 5:1–2). Like St. Paul in his address to the elders of Ephesus, St. Peter makes clear that each ministering man of whom he speaks is an elder, a shepherd (or pastor), and an overseer. All such ministers are in a position of great respect and leadership and supervise the spiritual lives of people and lead and feed them. Today we most frequently use the term pastor for those who are elders, overseers, and caretakers among us. The image of the shepherd (pastor) gives us abiding comfort, a sense of security, and great joy.

We are to honor our pastors. Of the elders Paul wrote to Timothy, "The elders who direct the affairs of the church well are worthy of double honor, especially those whose work is preaching and teaching" (1 Timothy 5:17). In giving honor to elders, we are to obey them as persons given authority by God so that they have joy in their work. "Obey your leaders and submit to their authority. They keep watch over you as men who must give an account. Obey them so that their work will be a joy, not a burden, for that would be of no advantage to you" (Hebrews 13:17). We are to "hold them in the highest regard in love because of their work" and "live in peace with each other" (1 Thessalonians 5:13). Also, we are to provide generously for the physical needs of the pastor and his family. We are to see to it that the pastor receives an appropriate and adequate salary. Paul writes, "Anyone who receives instruction in the word must share all good things with his instructor" (Galatians 6:6). In another place St. Paul writes concerning elders the Old Testament words, "The worker deserves his wages" (1 Timothy 5:18). God wants all His people to have joy, both His people and the pastors among them.

The pastors whom God gives to His church are first and foremost servants among the people of God. Jesus taught His disciples about the greatness of servanthood. One day He said to them, "The kings of the Gentiles lord it over them; and those who exercise authority over them call themselves Benefactors. But you are not to be like that. Instead, the greatest among you should be like the youngest, and the one who rules like the one who serves" (Luke 22:25–26).

5

The Pastor Has a Unique Role among the People of God

Pastors Have God-Assigned Tasks

God calls pastors to nurture His people in the parish as individuals, as groups, and as an entire congregation. We remember the words of St. Paul to the elders of Ephesus: "Keep watch over yourselves and all the flock of which the Holy Spirit has made you overseers. Be shepherds of the church of God, which he bought with his own blood" (Acts 20:28). St. Paul himself ministered to both individuals and groups of Christians. He wrote to Philemon for the benefit of one person, Onesimus; he cared for whole congregations such as those in Galatia and Corinth.

Second, God calls pastors to equip God's people for the Christian mission. St. Paul taught the Ephesians that pastors are to prepare God's people for works of service for the growth and maturity of the church. He wrote, "It was he [Christ] who gave some to be apostles, some to be prophets, some to be evangelists, and some to be pastors and teachers, to prepare God's people for works of service, so that the body of Christ may be built up until we all reach unity in the faith and in the knowledge of the Son of God and become mature, attaining to the whole measure of the fullness of Christ" (Ephesians 4:11–13).

In addition to equipping God's people for works of service, St. Paul also looked forward to himself being enabled for his work *by* God's people. He viewed enablement as a mutual thing. For example, Paul wrote to the Romans, "I long to see you so that I may impart to you some spiritual gift to make you strong—that is, that you and I may be mutually encouraged by each other's faith" (Romans 1:11–12).

Finally, God calls pastors to join the people of the church in the service of being Christ's presence in the world, especially in the task of bringing people to Christ and His church. Jesus directed His followers, "Go and make disciples of all nations" (Matthew 28:19). To them He said, "You will be my witnesses in Jerusalem, and in all Judea and Samaria, and to the ends of the earth" (Acts 1:8).

In summary, God calls pastors to nurture His people, to equip them for Christian service, and to join them in being Christlike servants to people of the world.

God Gives Pastors Authority for Word and Sacrament Ministry

God gives pastors the authority and the means necessary for fulfilling their work. He authorizes (gives authority to) them to carry out their tasks and to do their work in His place and in His stead by doing Word and Sacrament ministry. Thus, the pastor accomplishes God's purposes by proclaiming and teaching God's Word, Law and Gospel, and by administering the Sacraments of Baptism and the Lord's Supper. Everything the pastor does to nurture, equip, and pursue the work of evangelism is shaped and enabled by Word and Sacrament ministry.

We need only look at the New Testament to document the pastor's authority to do Word and Sacrament ministry. Jesus shared His authority with His disciples when He said, "All authority in heaven and on earth has been given to me. Therefore go and make disciples of all nations, baptizing them in the name of the Father and of the Son and of the Holy Spirit, and teaching them to obey everything I have commanded you. And surely I am with you always, to the very end of the age" (Matthew 28:18–20). Likewise, Jesus said to the apostles, "'As the Father has sent me, I am sending you.' And with that he breathed on them and said, 'Receive the Holy Spirit. If you forgive anyone his sins, they are forgiven; if you do not forgive them, they are not forgiven'" (John 20:21–23). On the night when He was betrayed, Jesus said to His disciples concerning the meal of His body and blood, "This is my body, which is for you; do this in remembrance of me. . . . This cup is the new covenant in my blood; do this, whenever you drink it, in remembrance of me" (1 Corinthians 11:24–25).

Concerning pastoral authority, we can add Paul's words to the young pastor Titus. St. Paul wrote that he should teach the message of salvation with all authority.

> For the grace of God that brings salvation has appeared to all men. It teaches us to say "No" to ungodliness and worldly passions, and to live self-controlled, upright and godly lives in this present age, while we wait for the blessed hope—

the glorious appearing of our great God and Savior, Jesus Christ, who gave himself for us to redeem us from all wickedness and to purify for himself a people that are his very own, eager to do what is good. These, then, are the things you should teach. Encourage and rebuke with all authority. (Titus 2:11–15)

The Pastor Is a Person of Authority for Edification

The purpose of the pastor's authority is to edify, that is, to build up the church. St. Paul boasted about the authority the Lord gave him for building up rather than tearing down. To the Corinthians he wrote, "Even if I boast somewhat freely about the authority the Lord gave us for building you up rather than pulling you down, I will not be ashamed of it" (2 Corinthians 10:8).

The Pastor's Authority Is the Authority of God's Word and the Authority of Serving

Let us be clear: The pastor has authority because he is given authority by Christ and shares in the authority of Christ. The pastor's authority among the people of God is the authority of God's Word and the authority of serving with, and according to, that Word under the lordship of Jesus Christ.

As the pastor serves faithfully, he expresses the authority of ministry. As he serves in the name of Christ, he demonstrates his authority. By God's design, such service is vested with its own authority. People recognize the pastor's authority in his serving in the name of Christ. They discern by his Word and Sacrament service that he is indeed a person of authority.

St. Paul is the model for pastors. He saw himself as an ambassador for Christ (2 Corinthians 5:18–21) who was "eager to preach the gospel" (Romans 1:14–17). He was dedicated to being a servant of God's people (2 Corinthians 4:5) and to setting forth the truth plainly to commend himself to every man's conscience in the sight of God (2 Corinthians 4:2–3).

We learn more about the pastor's authority when we talk about the authority of Jesus Himself. The Father gave all authority in heaven and earth to His Son, Jesus (Matthew 28:18–20). Jesus' authority was both the right and power to teach God's will and to act with God's power. Jesus had truth and power in Himself, and people recognized Him as the One who taught and acted with authority (Mark 1:22; Luke 4:31–32). First of all, Jesus acted with authorization from God as the One commissioned by God to speak for God because He was God. St. John writes, "No one has ever seen God, but God the One and Only, who is at the Father's side, has made him known" (John 1:18).

Furthermore, Jesus' authority was characterized by His strong sense of identity and by His display of competence, conviction, and confidence. He was a genuine and open person whose presence, words, and actions matched. "The people were amazed at his teaching, because he taught them as one who had authority, not as the teachers of the law" (Mark 1:22; see also Matthew 7:26–29; 9:1–8; Mark 1:21–28; Luke 4:31–36).

Fully understanding who He was and why He had come among us, Jesus served as a person with great power. Hear the words of St. John:

> Jesus knew that the Father had put all things under his power, and that he had come from God and was returning to God; so he got up from the meal, took off his outer clothing, and wrapped a towel around his waist. After that, he poured water into a basin and began to wash his disciples' feet, drying them with the towel that was wrapped around him. [Then Jesus said,] "I have set you an example that you should do as I have done for you. I tell you the truth, no servant is greater than his master, nor is a messenger greater than the one who sent him. Now that you know these things, you will be blessed if you do them." (John 13:3–5, 15–17)

The Father who endowed Jesus with authority gives authority to pastors to minister the Gospel to people in a variety of ways in order to restore them to His presence and power to be His own people who are outfitted to do good works (Matthew 28:16–20; 2 Corinthians 10:7–8; 5:18–21, 13:10; 1 Thessalonians 1; Titus 2:11–14). Then, so that they are capable of exercising their authority, God gives pastors power generated by the Holy Spirit (Acts 1:7–8). Thus pastors possess the power of the Holy Spirit and employ the power of the Gospel in exercising their authority (right) to minister, to serve. The authority of the pastor is both the right to act and the ability to act using the power of God.

According to God's design, pastors are to minister effectively. They are to proclaim and teach the Word of

God so that people can hear and understand God's message and the Holy Spirit can do His work in their lives. They are to serve in ways that make it possible for God's Gospel power to work in the lives for all kinds and conditions of people for the accomplishment of God's purposes. St. Paul had such a commitment. To the Corinthians he wrote:

> Though I am free and belong to no man, I make myself a slave to everyone, to win as many as possible. To the Jews I became like a Jew, to win the Jews. To those under the law I became like one under the law (though I myself am not under the law), so as to win those under the law. To those not having the law I became like one not having the law. . . . To the weak I became weak, to win the weak. I have become all things to all men so that by all possible means I might save some. I do all this for the sake of the gospel, that I may share in its blessings. (1 Corinthians 9:19–23)

For the pastor to be effective and joyful, his authority must be acknowledged, valued, and accepted by the people he serves. This was certainly true in the life of Jesus. His hearers recognized and accepted His authority to teach (Matthew 7:28–29; 9:1–8; Mark 1:22–27; 2:1–12; Luke 4:31–37; 5:17–26).

People accept, respect, and respond positively to the authority of the pastor as he lives among them in certain ways. First of all, people accept the pastor's authority when he lives among them as a person of competence, conviction, and confidence who possesses a strong sense of identity. Second, people accept the pastor's authority when he lives among them as a genuine and open person whose presence, words, and actions match. And finally, people accept the pastor's authority when he serves them with respect and high regard as members of the church who themselves have gifts and responsibility to participate in the decision-making processes and actions of the church. Also, they recognize that he trusts God's power to do its work as God wills and that he serves without seeking to control persons and events (1 Corinthians 3:5–9). According to God's design, this is the servant style by which the pastor, given right and power by God Himself, acquires among people their right regard to lead them and enable them to use God's grace for obedience to God's purposes. People look upon the pastor as the person sent by God to care for them as God's representative (Matthew 7:26–29; 1 Corinthians 9; 2 Corinthians 6:1–18; 2 Thessalonians 3:6–10). Pastors are to represent Christ among the people of God.

God Bids His People to Obey Leaders and Submit to Their Servant Authority

God wants His people to obey their spiritual leaders. He wants us to submit to their servant authority, so that we receive rich benefits from the service that God calls pastors to provide. The writer to the Hebrews has this to say: "Obey your leaders and submit to their authority. They keep watch over you as men who must give an account. Obey them so that their work will be a joy, not a burden, for that would be of no advantage to you" (Hebrews 13:17). To the Thessalonian Christians, St.

Paul wrote, "Now we ask you, brothers, to respect those who work hard among you, who are over you in the Lord and who admonish you. Hold them in the highest regard in love because of their work" (1 Thessalonians 5:12–13).

In the passage above, the writer to the Hebrews reminds us that the pastor in carrying out his office is accountable to Christ. St. Paul teaches the same truth. Writing to the Corinthians, Paul said, "So then, men ought to regard us as servants of Christ and as those entrusted with the secret things of God. Now it is required that those who have been given a trust must prove faithful. I care very little if I am judged by you or by any human court; indeed, I do not even judge myself. My conscience is clear, but that does not make me innocent. It is the Lord who judges me" (1 Corinthians 4:1–4).

The Pastor Facilitates a Shared Ministry

As an integral part of his service, the pastor facilitates a common and shared ministry. He sees to it that the people of God are not only equipped to use their gifts for the common good but also that they have opportunity and freedom to do their service as responsible Christians. So it must be if each Christian is to use his "manifestation of the Spirit" for the common good (1 Corinthians 12:6).

Just as the pastor facilitates a common and shared ministry between himself and God's people, so he also facilitates and participates in mutual accountability between himself and the people. Under Christ both pastor and people hold themselves accountable to one another for carrying out their responsibilities. The pastor is accountable to the people and the people are accountable to the pastor and to one another. They establish ways to carry out this accountability within the parish under the pastor's leadership. Not only did St. Paul say that pastors must prove faithful, but said to all the people, "Examine yourselves to see whether you are in the faith; test yourselves" (2 Corinthians 13:5). To the Ephesians Paul wrote, "Submit to one another out of reverence for Christ" (Ephesians 5:21).

Likewise, the pastor helps each and every person in the parish to be clear about roles and relationships. As a part of the accountability process, he assists the people on a continuing basis to evaluate the appropriateness of their roles and to adjust whatever needs to be adjusted in the areas of roles and relationships. St. Paul encourages the clarifying and evaluating of various roles and relationships. He does this in Ephesians 5 and 6 when he speaks to wives, husbands, children, slaves, and masters. He does the same in Colossians 3 and 1 Corinthians 12.

The Pastor Is a Model of Redeemed Humanness

In all that he does the pastor is a model of redeemed humanness. By his life he shows people how to live under the Law and Gospel as saint-and-sinner people. The pastor certainly does not reveal every private detail of his sinfulness, but he does not pretend to be perfect. When his sins are apparent he demonstrates repentance. He acknowledges his wrong and turns to God and

His people for forgiveness. This is not only the way the pastor is to live, but it is also the way people learn how to live the Christian life of daily repentance. They learn from the pastor's example. St. Paul showed us all this way of living when he wrote:

> So I find this law at work: When I want to do good, evil is right there with me. For in my inner being I delight in God's law; but I see another law at work in the members of my body, waging war against the law of my mind and making me a prisoner of the law of sin at work within my members. What a wretched man I am! Who will rescue me from this body of death? Thanks be to God—through Jesus Christ our Lord! (Romans 7:21–25)

When pastors are models of redeemed humanness, like St. Paul they can call people to be imitators of them.

6

God Has Joined Pastors and People Together to Share the Joy of God's Plan

God wants pastors and people to have joy in their life together. According to His design, God has joined people and pastors together to live and serve joyfully and effectively. God wants there to be joy in the parish—joy in living the life in Christ together and joy in carrying out God's purposes for His church.

St. Paul talks about joy in the parish. Of the joy of the members of the Thessalonian congregation Paul wrote, "You welcomed the message with the joy given by the Holy Spirit. And so you became a model to all the believers in Macedonia and Achaia" (1 Thessalonians 1:6–7). In turn, St. Paul spoke of the joy he received from his relationship with congregation in Thessalonica and described in detail what gave him joy. To them he wrote:

> Timothy has just now come to us from you and has brought good news about your faith and love. He has told us that you always have pleasant memories of us and that you long to see us, just as we also long to see you. Therefore, brothers, in all our distress and persecution we were encouraged about you because of your faith. For

now we really live, since you are standing firm in the Lord. How can we thank God enough for you in return for all the joy we have in the presence of our God because of you? (1 Thessalonians 3:6–9)

The Christians at Thessalonica had joy in the Gospel message St. Paul brought to them. Paul had joy in their faith, love, and steadfastness. Such is to be the joy of pastors and people.

Part 2

Causes for Joylessness
in the Parish

7

Indicators of Joylessness in the "Clergy Shortage Study"

Because of a present and projected shortage of clergy in The Lutheran Church—Missouri Synod, its Board for Higher Education commissioned a "Clergy Shortage Study" that was submitted at the close of 1999. This study incorporated interviews with a large variety of people, including spokespersons of other denominations. Among those interviewed in The Lutheran Church—Missouri Synod were parish pastors, pastors' wives, pastors' children, university and seminary students, wives of seminary students, and District presidents.

The "Clergy Shortage Study" reveals powerful indicators of joylessness in many parishes. These indicators are expressed in the problems identified by the researchers. Some that seem especially relevant to our concerns are as follows:

- Both pastors and people spend a lot of time verbally and emotionally beating up on each other.

- Many pastors live at or near the poverty level.

- People have unrealistic expectations of pastors who in turn are attempting to do entirely too much, neglecting themselves and their families.

- Large numbers of congregations fight within themselves. These sick congregations chew up and spit out pastor after pastor.

- In some congregations a few members dominate the majority. These strong-willed individuals hold the majority of the members hostage to their personal point of view; they abuse pastors and run them off.

- A significant number of people are entering the ministry for the wrong reason—to fix all that is wrong in congregations.

- People are entering the ministry when they have no other options.

- About 40 percent of LCMS pastors are either depressed or burned out or are approaching those conditions.

- A large number of parish pastors daily display a profession filled with pain, depression, abuse, neglect of family, and stress.

- Parents degrade their pastor in the hearing of their children.

8

Pastors' Wrong Understandings and Behaviors that Diminish Joy

Pastors Sometimes Seek to Control People

Pastors sometimes fail to pursue the togetherness of pastor and people as God envisions such togetherness. Pastors occasionally seek to control people and events out of their personal need and for their personal advantage. Knowingly or unknowingly, they attempt to meet their personal needs by being authoritarian rather than authoritative, by being legalistic rather than evangelical.

St. Peter talks about pastors who feel they *must* serve as overseers rather than serving willingly. Rather than being eager to serve, they may work because they are "greedy for money." Instead of being examples to the flock, they may lord it over those entrusted to them (1 Peter 5:2–3).

In his Letter to the Philippians Paul speaks about "some [who] preach Christ out of envy and rivalry" and "out of selfish ambition" (Philippians 1:15–17). In another letter, St. Paul observes that pastors might possibly aim to please other people and to "win the approval of men" (Galatians 1:10). The prophet Ezekiel

warned the shepherds of Israel not to take care of themselves at the expense of taking care of the flock (Ezekiel
4:11–13).

Pastors Sometimes Fail to Equip Others for Service

Pastors often do facets of ministry but fail to equip
and facilitate the service of God's people. The pastor is
called to do public ministry. This means His ministry is
to proclaim the Word and administer the Sacraments
for God's people and on their behalf. He is the public
minister. However, as we have seen, the pastor is not the
only person in the parish who has ministry to do. All of
God's people have service to perform. The pastor's
responsibility is to enable them to do the work of their
service.

Unfortunately, pastors at times do their Word and
Sacrament ministry and additional tasks, too, that
rightly belong to members of the congregation. They do
not equip God's people for their work of service, encourage them to serve, or provide them with opportunities
to carry out their ministry. Such pastors do, or try to do,
everything that has to be done in the congregation.
Both pastors and people need to recall the words of St.
Paul that pastors are to "prepare God's people for works
of service" (Ephesians 4:11–12).

Pastors Want to Look Correct

Pastors sometimes lose sight of their calling by trying to look correct rather than striving authentically to
live and model the Christian life. When they do, they

give parishioners a false notion of what Christianity is all about, and they make themselves emotionally unavailable to people. People are reluctant to turn for help to pastors who seem to be less than partners in the Christian struggle against sin. In turn, when the pastor wants to look right and righteous at all times, parishioners seem to take less seriously what he has to say because he seems distant from their life experience. They experience him as paternalistic, pedantic, and condescending when he talks to others.

To the Corinthians St. Paul spoke about men who wanted to appear better than they actually were. Paul wrote, "I will keep on doing what I am doing in order to cut the ground from under those who want an opportunity to be considered equal with us in the things they boast about. For such men are false apostles, deceitful workmen, masquerading as apostles of Christ" (2 Corinthians 11:12–13).

9

People's Wrong Under-standings and Behaviors that Diminish Joy

God's people sometimes fail to pursue the together-ness that generates joy. There are people of the parish who prefer to be onlookers and receivers rather than participants. They fail to use the pastor as God's servant-overseer and equipper. They take from the pastor only what they want when they want it. They display a consumer mentality.

St. Paul has words that reflect the need for parish-ioners to use their pastors as God's representatives for their spiritual growth and service.

> Now we ask you, brothers, to respect those who work hard among you, who are over you in the Lord and who admonish you. Hold them in the highest regard in love because of their work. Live in peace with each other. And we urge you, brothers, warn those who are idle, encourage the timid, help the weak, be patient with everyone. (1 Thessalonians 5:12–14)

Unfortunately, people of the parish face, and often succumb to, the temptation to treat the pastor like an employee. They criticize him and attempt to control him for their own purposes. Some even become antagonists who are unreasonable and unrelenting in attempting to get rid of the pastor.

Today there are still people like those who made St. Paul's ministry difficult. To the Galatians, he spoke of people who "are zealous to win you over, but for no good. What they want is to alienate you from us, so that you may be zealous for them. It is fine to be zealous, provided the purpose is good, and to be so always and not just when I am with you" (Galatians 4:17–18). When St. Paul wrote to the Corinthians, he gave this advice: "I appeal to you, brothers, in the name of our Lord Jesus Christ, that all of you agree with one another so that there may be no divisions among you and that you may be perfectly united in mind and thought" (1 Corinthians 1:10). St. Paul knew what it was like for someone to be antagonistic. He told the young pastor Timothy, "Alexander the metalworker did me a great deal of harm. The Lord will repay him for what he has done. You too should be on your guard against him, because he strongly opposed our message" (2 Timothy 4:14–15).

10

Non-Christian Behaviors that Destroy Faithfulness and Joy

Disobedience to God's plan for His people erodes faithfulness and joy among pastors and people. It produces harmful competitiveness, personal and interpersonal hurt, and unfaithfulness in carrying forward the purposes of God.

Pastors, on their part, feel unrewarded, misunderstood, abused, angry, afraid, betrayed, lonely, burned out and they often respond by behaving inappropriately. They frequently become depressed and try to control people and activities more aggressively and sometimes become involved in self-destructive behaviors.

We have biblical examples of hurtful behaviors born of fear, personal ambition, and greed. Peter denied Jesus (Luke 25:55–57). Judas betrayed Jesus (Matthew 26:47–49). James and John, the sons of Zebedee, wanted to sit at Jesus' right and left hands in His glory (Mark 10:35–37).

Like pastors, parishioners can exhibit a variety of inappropriate and hurtful attitudes and behaviors. They experience hurt, anger, fear, and detachment. They sometimes become antagonists determined to get rid of the pastor. We remember again the experience of St. Paul at the hands of people who were against him. Demas deserted Paul. Alexander did him great harm.

When Paul stood trial, no one came to his support. To the contrary, everyone deserted him (2 Timothy 4:10–16). Members of the congregation in Corinth sought to discredit Paul and his ministry. Today people still try to get rid of pastors, do them greater harm, and fail to support their ministry. However, as we shall discover, pastors and people can indeed live and grow together in joy. God provides all we need for joy in the parish.

Part 3

Concepts for Increasing and Maintaining Joy in the Parish

11

Concepts from Family Systems Theory

When faced with problems we rely first and last upon the means of grace that God has provided: the Word of God and the Holy Sacraments. Through these, God administers the forgiveness of sins to flawed human beings. Through these means of grace God also brings the healing balm of the Holy Spirit into conflicted human relationships, with the result that there is joy in the parish. We have seen how God's Word helps us analyze the problem, and later will explore more fully how Scripture provides solid guidance and practical teaching—all centered in the grace of God in Christ—to conflicted pastors and congregations.

In His goodness God also has provided us with valid insights and understandings from a variety of disciplines, such as the findings of human behavior research and the perspectives of health care professionals. Such insights, when compatible with the truths of Scripture, can assist us, by the power of the Gospel, to increase and maintain joy in the parish.

In recent years religious writers have applied family systems thinking to life in religious congregations. Among these writers are the late Edwin Friedman in *Generation to Generation: Family Process in Church and Synagogue* (1985) and also Peter Steinke in *How Your Church Family Works* (1993).

Some of the basic concepts of family systems theory provide us with concepts, consistent with biblical thought, for increasing and maintaining joy in the parish. I have selected several of them for our review. These are self-differentiation, nonanxious presence, balance, process and content, overfunctioning, emotional triangles, and symptom bearer. What is true of family systems is true of congregational families and of all systems for that matter.

Self-Differentiation

According to Friedman, "differentiation means the capacity of a family member to define his or her own life's goals and values apart from surrounding togetherness pressures, to say 'I' when others are demanding 'you' and 'we' " (p. 27). It is especially important for a person in a leadership position to define his goals and take responsibility for his position while, at the same time, keeping in touch with the ideas, attitudes, and feelings of others in the group of which he himself is a member. The leader is an emotionally available person who seeks to be responsive and not reactive as he moves the group he leads toward its goals.

How important is self-differentiation on the part of the pastor and other congregational leaders? Friedman writes, "The overall health and functioning of any organization depend primarily on one or two people at the top. . . . The key to successful spiritual leadership, therefore, with success understood not only as moving people toward a goal, but also in terms of the survival of the family (and its leader) has more to do with the leader's capacity for self-definition than with the ability to motivate others" (Friedman, p. 22).

Nonanxious Presence

As a well-defined person, every member of a group, especially the leader or leaders, needs to cultivate and maintain a nonanxious presence, especially in the midst of group anxiety. The capacity to be nonanxious, in connection with personal differentiation, is an essential and powerful quality, especially for leaders. An individual's nonanxious presence facilitates clearheadedness and appropriate action and reduces anxiety in the group.

Balance

The concept of balance suggests that a family or family-type group seeks to keep a balance. The balance may be functional or dysfunctional, but it is a balance to which the network of relationships has become accustomed. This means that personal families or congregational families feel secure when they practice their customary patterns of interaction. Even when the patterns are counterproductive or painful, members of the relationship network will struggle to maintain or return to usual patterns of interaction.

The concept of balance is important in family systems theory because family systems theory believes that unresolved relational problems of individuals, rather than the makeup of individual personalities, disturb balance. Unresolved problems significantly influence our relationships and how we function in our relationships. This means that achieving and maintaining balance within the structure of relationships is of great importance, especially when changes take place in the life of the group or the lives of individual members of the group.

It may seem as though imbalance problems in the network of relationships are caused by new ideas or philosophies. But this is not the case. Generally they reflect unresolved personal issues of members. For example, writes Friedman, "In congregations that have long been run by a few families, the conflict in the congregation can, as in a family business, appear to be about new ideas or a change in philosophy. but the intensity can really reflect personal issues in those families, particularly intergenerational problems between father and son" (p. 203).

Process and Content

As already observed, imbalance in the congregation often is seen as related to content, that is, content issues, ideas, or philosophies. But, as suggested, Friedman believes that this is not the case. Rather, he contends, issues and ideas are handled rationally and through the democratic process when the relationship system is in balance. Imbalance, then, is often not caused by content but is the result of unresolved emotional issues on the part of members of the group. This can be true of criticism directed toward spiritual leaders. "Every time members of a congregation begin to concentrate on their minister's 'performance,' there is a good chance they are displacing something from their own personal lives" (p. 208).

Friedman's approach calls us to focus less on content and more on process when the congregation experiences imbalance. He concludes, "To the extent a symptom goes away because the complaining party was appeased, or where issues are resolved in isolation from other changes in the system, such change is not likely to last" (p. 207).

Even though Friedman's belief is that we are to focus less on content and more on process when there is imbalance within a congregation, this does not mean, even to Friedman, that content is never a serious issue. To the contrary, as we shall discuss in more detail later, content may very much be an issue for attention.

Overfunctioning

The concept of overfunctioning applies here primarily to the pastor. Pastors often feel that they are stuck with all the responsibility in the congregation and with the heavy obligation of getting other people to be responsible. Friedman observes that "overfunctioning in any system is an anxious response in both senses of the word, 'anxious' as in anticipatory and 'anxious' as in *fearful*" (p. 211). Overfunctioning is an expression of anxiety and also a promoter of anxiety. When a pastor is overfunctional he courts burnout and opens himself to forces that erode his spiritual life. The ministry becomes a burden, not a service of joy.

Emotional Triangles

Concerning the concept of emotional triangles, Friedman writes,

> The basic law of emotional triangles is that when any two parts of a system become uncomfortable with one another, they will "triangle in" or focus upon a third person, or issue, as a way of stabilizing their own relationship with one another. A person may be said to be "triangled" if he or she

gets caught in the middle of the focus of such an unresolved issue. Conversely, when individuals try to change the relationship of two others (two people, or a person, and his or her symptom or belief), they "triangle" themselves into that relationship (and often stabilize the very situation they are trying to change). (pp. 35–36)

How can we deal with triangles? Sometimes it is important for us to stay out of or get out of triangles. However, it seems possible to facilitate change in the relationship of two others if, as a person involved in the relationship, we maintain a well-defined relationship with each person and avoid taking responsibility for their relationship with each other. Friedman writes, "To the extent we can maintain 'nonanxious presence' in a triangle, such a stance has the potential to modify the anxiety in the others. The problem is to be nonanxious and present" (p. 39). Otherwise, we end up with the stress of the other two parties of the triangle and see little or no resolution to relationship problems.

Symptom Bearer or Identified Patient

When a member of a system (family or congregation) is identified as a patient, a person with serious problems, that person is actually the symptom bearer. His unacceptable behavior is a sign of serious problems in the system. He is the person in whom the family's stresses or unresolved issues have surfaced.

Friedman offers some examples of possible symptoms of the identified patient. He gives these observations:

In a child it could take the form of excessive bed wetting, hyperactivity, school failures, drugs, obesity, or juvenile diabetes; in a spouse its form could be excessive drinking, depression, chronic ailments, a heart condition or perhaps even cancer; in an aged member of the family it could show up as confusion, senility, or agitated and random behavior. In a congregational family it could surface as the drinking, burnout, or sexual acting out of the "family leader." (p. 19)

The concept of the symptom bearer or identified patient shows clearly that the problems of one person are in reality the problems of the system. The entire system needs to be addressed in order to bring healing. The system needs to be brought into healthy balance by addressing process concerns. The family systems way of thinking focuses on emotional process rather than symptomatic content and advocates eliminating symptoms by modifying the structure of the system rather than attempting to change the dysfunctional part directly.

12

Concepts from the Field of Addictions

Like family systems thinking, addictions research offers insights to help us advance and sustain joy in the parish. Many of these understandings correlate with those of family systems theory.

The field of addictions addresses people's destructive loss of control over substances and/or behaviors of body and mind, also called process addictions. Some substances to which people become addicted are alcohol, cocaine, marijuana, nicotine, caffeine, and food. Some processes to which people become addicted are gambling, work, and sex.

Persons who are addicted to substances and/or behaviors have many unresolved emotional and relational issues as well as physical ills. They are dysfunctional persons who severely disturb the balance of every system of which they are a part, also the congregation. They are anxious persons who lack self-differentiation.

Addicted persons bring chaos to relationships. They are unpredictable, deny their addiction(s), blame their woes on others, and are masters at manipulating others to their advantage. They create imbalance in their interpersonal relationships. They need the attention of all the systems to which they belong, and the systems to which they belong need attention. Dysfunctional systems have their way of perpetuating addictions whatever their cause may be, and systems must be involved in the healing processes for the sake of both the system and the addicted person.

One particular phenomenon discussed among people in the field of addictions has a significant contribution to make to our discussion of joy in the parish. This is the concept of codependency. Codependency is defined in different ways by different people. Actually, codependence is itself an addiction. Sharon Wegscheider-Cruse speaks of codependence as an addiction to another person or persons or to a relationship and its problems. Howard Clinebell talks about codependence in a similar way when he observes that codependents are caregivers who are dependent on the dependence of addicted people. They seek to help addicted persons by attempting to control them, by protecting them from the consequences of their behavior, and by taking responsibility for their harmful ways of behaving.

In my book *When Addictions Threaten*, I characterize codependent persons as follows:

> Codependent persons are overly responsible. They feel responsible for life's problems and taking care of others. They have an intense drive to control the behavior of others with guilt and manipulation. In turn, they have a sense of low self-esteem and self-worth; they feel ashamed of themselves and put others first in their lives to their own detriment. Whatever feelings of self-worth they may have come from helping others. Interpersonal relationships are difficult for codependents. They have difficulty trusting others, knowing what is normal in life, and asking for

what they need from others. They tend to fear
abandonment and seek love from people who are
unable to give it to them. Many codependents
marry alcoholics and other addicts. Some become
alcoholics and suffer from a variety of addictions.
(p. 27)

Other notable characteristics of codependents
include perfectionism, self-criticism, rigid "black and
white" thinking, and difficulty working with others.
Codependents are experts at vagueness and niceness.
They look like loving and giving persons but frequently
are angry, depressed, strongly controlling, and manipu-
lative.

An addiction familiar to codependents, and born
out of codependency, is the addiction to work, often
called workaholism. A work addict is a person who
thinks about work all the time. He finds work stimulat-
ing and is unable to do without the excitement of work.
This kind of behavior is akin to the overfunctioning discussed above in connection with family systems theory.

Codependents experience deep pain in their lives.
As a way of dealing with their pain, they often become
members of the helping professions—including the
ministry—and work with people to satisfy their own
personal needs. Fortunately, it is not necessary to be so
driven. God is able to break this unhealthy cycle. As will
be seen, the insights of psychology and the truths of
Holy Scripture provide suggestions for increasing and
maintaining joy in the parish.

Part 4

Suggestions for Increasing and Maintaining Joy in the Parish

13

Suggestions from Family Systems Theory

The concepts of family systems theory we have reviewed offer us suggestions for increasing and maintaining joy in the parish. These suggestions are consistent with, and supportive of, what we have learned from Scripture about the life together of pastors and people.

Self-Differentiation

Family systems theory suggests that every member of the parish, pastor and people alike, should aim to be self-differentiated. Peter Steinke is very helpful in summing up the meaning of self-differentiation. He writes that self-differentiation is

—defining yourself and staying in touch with others;

—being responsible for yourself and responsive to others;

—maintaining your integrity and well-being without intruding on that of others;

—allowing the enhancement of the other's integrity and well-being without feeling abandoned, inferior, or less a self;

—having an "I" and entering a relationship with another without losing yourself or diminishing the self of others. (p. 11)

In short, according to Steinke, "self-differentiation means 'being separate together' or 'being connected selves' " (p. 11). Important for self and others, the self-differentiated person stays in touch with what is going on in the lives of others and what others think, feel, and want. He is emotionally available to others without being undifferentiated by them. He highly regards others, has empathy for them, and relates to them as a genuine person whose presence, words, and actions match. He does not use his determination to be self-differentiated as an excuse for doing otherwise.

Persons like Jesus and St. Paul commend themselves to us as being self-differentiated persons. They serve as models for all of us and especially for pastors who serve as leaders of Christian congregations. It is vital for us to strive for the differentiation of ourselves and to support one another in this pursuit. Such self-differentiation, especially on the part of the pastor, facilitates change and joy within the congregational system. The lack of it hinders the church in carrying out its mission. It produces imbalance among the people of God and diminishes joy in the parish.

Nonanxious Presence

Being self-differentiated includes being non-anxiously present among others. It is a necessary ingredient in self-differentiation. Anxiety in itself is not bad. Rather, anxiety can be creative and produce change. It can energize us for positive action. However, when anxiety becomes intense, it is counterproductive. It prevents the change and progress that it intends to facilitate. Again, pastors and people alike have the challenge before them to be nonanxiously present among one another. This can be a blessing for all in living and serving together. St. Paul advised such a posture when he wrote, "Do not be anxious about anything, but in everything, by prayer and petition, with thanksgiving, present your requests to God. And the peace of God, which transcends all understanding, will guard your hearts and your minds in Christ Jesus" (Philippians 4:6–7).

Process and Content

Functional balance within the congregation is to be earnestly desired in the maintenance of joy. Thus, congregational leaders and members need to be alert to changes in their personal and family lives that might cause dysfunction in the congregation's network of relationships. When problems arise in the congregation or we are inclined to complain about this or that, we sometimes need to look for the motivation in process rather than content. Perhaps we will find the underlying causes of imbalance and complaints in personal problems, dramatic life changes, or unresolved emotional issues rather than ideas or philosophies. We can often bring about changes in the system by changing the way we relate to others. The resulting temporary upset often effects fundamental change in due time.

However, as Friedman himself suggests, there are times when attention to content is necessary before fundamental change can be realized. When Martin Luther opposed the church authorities of his day, he was genuinely dealing with content. He was upholding the Gospel, the true treasure of the church, not working out unresolved issues with his father.

Nevertheless, imbalance in a congregation may frequently be created by process more than content, process that needs priority attention. When we experience such imbalance, we do need to consider seriously the possibility of unresolved emotional issues, as well as the significance of conflicting ideas and perspectives. Why not take a look at it? We need to be wise and discerning.

Peter Steinke offers us these insightful and challenging words:

> The church family has its "distancers" in the non-active and quitters. It has its share of "fusers" who consider the church family to be their property. Moreover, people act out of their own unfinished agendas in other relationships with members of the congregation. Some are intent on haranguing others so that they don't have to change themselves. Some are forever cheating others of their birthright for their own special place in the family. Still others form a crankiness crowd, looking for external conditions that explain their own unhappiness. And what church family doesn't have a sunshine squad? Fearful of differences and differing, they brighten the family's life and distract it from threatening storm clouds. (p. 38)

Overfunctioning

The concept of overfunctioning is related to anxiety. Anxious persons are often overfunctioning, and by their overfunctioning they intensify anxiety for themselves and people around them. For a pastor to be overfunctioning is hurtful for him, his own family, and members of the parish. He takes on more responsibility than his ministry requires and than his health can sustain. In turn, he prevents others from being responsible for themselves and their Christian service.

Members of the parish can also be overfunctioning and thus adversely affect themselves and other members of the congregation. Parishioners need to be on the alert for overfunctioning in their lives and in the parish and do what they can to discourage the pastor from being overly responsible. They need to act responsibly but not be overly responsible in the interest of joy in the parish.

Emotional Triangles

Both pastors and people need to be watchful that they do not express their extreme and painful anxiety by triangling. It is so easy for us to do. For example, when George and Bill are having problems in their relationship, the more anxious of the two (George) involves a third person (Richard) to reduce the anxiety between Bill and himself. George may blame Richard for the problems between Bill and himself and/or he may try to make Richard feel responsible for solving their problems. Quite likely Richard will come to feel more anxiety and stress than either George or Bill.

The other side of the coin is that we need to keep ourselves not only from triangling but also from being triangled. Pastors and lay leaders in a congregation need to be especially careful about being triangled and how they deal with such involvement if it happens.

What are some of the scenarios of triangling that might take place in the parish to lessen joy?

1. A member may experience a painful life crisis and in his anxiety begin to criticize the pastor. Even

though the anxiety has to do with other relationships, the member in crisis focuses on the pastor.

2. On the way out of church one Sunday a member says to the pastor, "Have you heard what some people are saying about you? They are saying that . . ." This member is actually dealing with his own feelings, but he tries to hide his own thoughts and feelings and involve the pastor by referring to "some people."

3. The pastor wants to chant in the worship service, but the congregation disapproves. Thus the pastor asks the director of music to have the choir members put pressure on the congregation members to approve chanting.

Symptom Bearer or Identified Patient

The third person in a triangle is the person who ends up with anxiety and stress. This person is called the "symptom bearer" or "identified patient." Sometimes that person is known as the "burden bearer" or "scapegoat."

There can also be an "identified problem." Steinke offers this explanation:

> In some cases I have also found an "identified problem." Whenever a certain church family is anxious, it focuses it anxiety on the same spot— "the budget," or "the bishop," or "the past," or "the unfriendliness." Many times the identified problem is the pastoral office. In fact, some church families have a history of shifting their burden to the pastor. The source of the burden may not have much to do with the pastor. Yet

these systems focus their anxiety on that position.
It is automatic. It is their norm for regaining sta-
bility. (p. 49)

To avoid becoming symptom bearers we need to
practice what we have discussed. Here we need to focus
on process and not just on content. We need to be alert
and competent in dealing with triangles.

From family systems theory we obtain many suggestions for pastors and people in joyfully living their
life together and carrying out the mission of the church.
These are suggestions that assist us in living as God's
people as Scripture teaches us to live.

14

Suggestions from the Field of Addictions

Like our consideration of family systems understandings, our previous brief overview of addictions offers significant suggestions with regard to our interest in enlarging and sustaining joy in the parish.

As we have already affirmed, addictions are destructive. They crush joy. They destroy persons and everyone associated with them. Thus it is vitally important for pastors and parishioners to understand the nature and consequences of addictions and how to foster recovery.

When the pastor or members of a congregation suffer from one or more addictions, those associated with them must be careful not to deny, minimize, or facilitate the addictions. Rather, we must join together to enable the addicted person to acknowledge his hurtful behavior and obtain treatment. We ourselves are to participate in that treatment and recovery process for our sakes and for the sake of the recovering person and the entire fellowship. The words of the writer to the Hebrews encourage us: "Let us throw off everything that hinders and the sin that so easily entangles, and let us run with perseverance the race marked out for us. Let us fix our eyes on Jesus, the author and perfecter of our faith" (Hebrews 12:1–2).

More information about addictions and recovery from addictions is found in my two CPH books, *The*

Twelve Steps: The Church's Challenge and Opportunity and *When Addictions Threaten.*

The concept of codependence is relevant to our interest in increasing and maintaining joy in the parish. Codependent behavior, like every addiction, powerfully crushes joy.

It is has been suggested that 96 percent of the population is codependent to some degree. That may be true, but here we are concerned about people who are severely codependent and intensely dysfunctional, at least codependent enough for them to be joyless and diminish joy in the parish by thwarting God's saving plan for His people and the world.

Considering what codependency is and what the characteristics of codependency are, pastors and people who live together in parishes need to examine themselves to discover whether or not they are codependent. If we acknowledge codependency, we need to discover to what extent and in what ways we are codependent and seek to recover in the Christian ways I have discussed in my book *When Addictions Threaten.*

When we compare the insights and cautions of family systems theory with those characterizing codependence, we can readily recognize that codependent persons have the attributes of those people, pastors and parishioners alike, who have serious problems related to achieving self-differentiation and nonanxious presence and to dealing with triangles. In many ways we are looking at different sides of the same coin.

Overfunctioning in the form of work addiction is often a problem for codependents that contributes to joylessness. The work-addicted person, or workaholic, thinks about work all the time and cannot do without the excitement and stimulation of work. When he is not working or planning his work, the workaholic is often depressed. He needs the increase in energy that he receives when he works.

There is no joy in work addiction for the addict and those close to him. Workaholism threatens physical and emotional well-being and hurts people in every group to which the addicted person belongs.

Many pastors, as well as parishioners, are addicted to work. They need to be in touch with persons who can assist them in recovering from their dependency.

While the suggestions we offer apply to all members of the parish, young and old alike, they are of special significance to pastors. A pastor who is seriously code-pendent simply cannot carry out his ministry as mandated by God. He cannot serve among God's people if he has a sense of low self-esteem, a strong desire to control others, and a compulsion to serve only to meet his own personal needs. This does not mean that codependent persons should not enter the ministry. They have experiences that will serve them well in ministering to others. However, they must identify their codependent attitudes and behaviors and turn to God for his forgiving and life-changing help in order to transform those attitudes and behaviors into attitudes and behaviors that are useful to God and produce joy.

To move us toward recovery from everything that hinders us, St. Paul writes, "I urge you, brothers, in view of God's mercy, to offer your bodies as living sacrifices, holy and pleasing to God—this is your spiritual act of worship. Do not conform any longer to the pattern of this world, but be transformed by the renewing of your mind. Then you will be able to test and approve what God's will is—his good, pleasing and perfect will" (Romans 12:1–2). God in His grace can bring healing in this area. Ask Him for help. He will surely answer.

15

Suggestions for the Mutual Growth of Pastors and People

As we have observed, family systems thinking and addictions research offer us insights and suggestions for dealing with parish problems. Ultimately, however, we rely on the divine and eternal truths revealed in the Bible to evaluate the validity and usefulness of such insights and suggestions and to direct us in the way we are to go. To Scripture, then, we turn again for God's advice and for His enabling aid and assistance.

God has truly joined pastors and people together to live and serve joyfully in their togetherness. However, both pastors and people sometimes fail to pursue togetherness. We sometimes behave in less-than-Christian ways, hurt one another, and become unfaithful in carrying out God's purposes. Nevertheless, there is good news. Pastors and people can grow in the togetherness designed for them by God. We do this by

- living under God's love and life-renewing power in Word and Sacrament;

- reviewing together and affirming God's plan for the church: the mission-directed togetherness of pastor and people;

- engaging in open and trusting dialog to identify and confess our misunderstandings, wrong deeds, and concerns, and, when appropriate, by using the help of communication facilitators and reconcilers;

• embracing God's forgiveness in Word and Sacrament and sharing His forgiveness and our forgiveness with one another and by encouraging one another;

• continually promoting competence in one another for faithfulness to God's purposes, using, when appropriate, programs designed to equip God's people for service; and

• planning and making decisions together about the affairs of the church.

We grow as Christians because God Himself provides growth through the Word and Sacraments; He personally instructs and empowers us. St. Peter assures us that the living and enduring Word of God is the pure spiritual milk by which we grow up in our salvation (1 Peter 1:22–23). St. Paul teaches us that we are one as we all share in the same bread in the Lord's Supper (1 Corinthians 10:17).

Ultimately, we grow as Christians as we live under the forgiveness of God and practice forgiveness in our relationships with one another. We recognize that each one of us is both a forgiven person and a sinner. We daily sin much even as we strive to live our new life in Christ. We daily need God's forgiveness and a new supply of His Holy Spirit. In turn, we need to forgive others just as we need their forgiveness. Nor is this impossible; it is altogether possible. We can be both forgiven and forgiving because of Jesus Christ. He has purchased and won us from all sins, their condemnation and power over us. He has done this by suffering the punishment due us for our sins. He did this when He, the Son of God, died on the cross. As St. Paul writes, we are able to "be kind and compassionate to one another, forgiving each other, just as in Christ God forgave you" (Ephesians 4:32).

Practicing mutual forgiveness in our life together restores our relationships when they became fragile and fractured. It restores relationships so that we can learn from the past, grow together, and not be stuck in our old sinful ways of behaving. It provides us with new opportunities and resources to live together in mutual care and work together in carrying out our Christian mission. In God's forgiveness and our mutual forgiveness we find joy.

Part 5

Recommendations for Pastors for Joyful Ministry and Personal Growth

16

Recommendations for Pastors concerning Pastoral Authority

Pastors frequently have problems in the parish because either they or their parishioners, or both, do not clearly understand the nature of pastoral authority as we have discussed it on the basis of Scripture. Both pastors and people have the potential for abusing pastoral authority. Their abuse causes both the discontent and dissension in Christian congregations that has intensified in recent years.

Our challenge as pastors is to shape a biblical understanding of pastoral authority and to minister out of that understanding. As we do, we will certainly minister faithfully and effectively. In turn, the people of the congregation will experience pastoral authority in ways that enable them to respond by shaping for themselves an accurate understanding of pastoral authority and rightly to relate to it.

In shaping a correct concept of pastoral authority, we need to affirm that the authority Jesus has given us is the authority to serve people with the Gospel (Law and Gospel) according to God's Word. True authority reveals itself by ministry. Self-giving ministry is the essential characteristic of authority. To serve means that we faithfully and competently proclaim and teach the

Word of God and administer the Sacraments among people.

We are to avoid seeking to control people and events for our own self-serving purposes. We are to avoid authoritarianism and legalism. We have enough to do, and be joyful about, in applying Law and Gospel to the lives of people, so that they grow by God's empowering grace and have opportunity to shape their lives and the congregation's life according to the Gospel.

If we believe some decision or action on the part of God's people does not serve the Gospel, or is even contrary to the Word of God, we do well to be patient with them by discussing the matter with them evangelically over a period of time. Unless there are compelling reasons to the contrary, we need to do our leading and feeding patiently. It is often difficult to discern accurately what motivates the attitudes and actions of people. Sometimes they may lack information or have wrong information. At times their behavior may reflect unresolved problems in their personal lives. They may not be intentionally disobedient.

When people of the congregation choose to do something with which we as pastors do not agree for personal reasons, we should not seek forcibly to control their actions. Rather we should lead them and join them in reviewing pros and cons of the matter with a view to the purposes of the church. All involved (or a majority of involved persons), including the pastor, may decide that the plan is indeed good and go forward with it. On the other hand, those involved (or a majority of those involved) may discover that what they are doing, or want to do, does not or will not well serve the mission of the church. Then they can alter their decision and apply what they have learned to future times of decision making.

Having patience with people does not mean that we should overlook people's persistently disobedient or mean-spirited behavior. For their sake and the sake of others, we cannot let people do whatever they want. We are to speak the truth of the Law to them lovingly and firmly; we are to confront them so that they can confront themselves (Luke 3:7–9; 6:24–26; 11:37–54). In turn, we have the right and responsibility to protect ourselves and our ministry from people's bad intentions (Mark 3:20–30; Luke 4:28–30; John 6:14–15). Here we may find the advice of Friedman and Steinke very helpful.

As pastors we do well to remember that we cannot change people. Only God can change them through the Gospel we proclaim. But we can change ourselves by making use of God's grace in our lives and perhaps thereby facilitate change in the lives of others.

It is wise for us not to use our energy trying to control events and people. Rather, let us give free reign to the power of God by speaking the truth (both Law and Gospel) in love so that people will hear the truth and the Holy Spirit can work powerfully through the Word of truth. Let us find the joy of ministry in serving others with the Word and Sacraments. For this we are called. Surely we will have ample opportunities to say to people of God the very words that St. Paul wrote to the Thessalonians:

We always thank God for all of you, mentioning you in our prayers. We continually remember before our God and Father your work produced by faith, your labor prompted by love, and your endurance inspired by hope in our Lord Jesus Christ. For we know, brothers loved by God, that he has chosen you, because our gospel came to you not simply with words, but also with power, with the Holy Spirit and with deep conviction. (1 Thessalonians 1:2–5)

17

Recommendations for Pastors about Growth and Support in Ministry

It is a large challenge for many pastors to maintain a self-differentiated, nonanxious presence in the practice of pastoral ministry, especially in the face of uncertainty, conflict, and antagonism.

As a pastor myself, I have learned from experience that it is necessary for pastors to participate fervently in the Word and Sacrament life of the Christian congregation and to take part fully in the mutual care of Christ's people, not only giving but also receiving care. Likewise, pastors need to permit God to support us and foster our personal spiritual growth by maintaining a rich devotional life centered in the use of God's Word and the privilege of prayer.

It is important for us as pastors intentionally to participate in one or more support relationships and/or groups to maintain a self-differentiated, nonanxious, change-facilitating presence in the congregation.

There are a number of possibilities.

1. Regular use of the means of grace, especially private Confession and Absolution.

2. Informal supportive relationships with pastors or other professionals.

3. A formal supportive and guiding and mentoring

relationship with another professional—a pastoral counselor, CPE (Clinical Pastoral Education) supervisor, or a Christian psychotherapist.

4. Formal support groups made up of

a. congregational leaders;

b. fellow pastors, perhaps in circuit conferences;

c. fellow pastors who meet regularly for mutual support and the guidance of a professional therapist, such as a pastoral counselor or psychotherapist, a CPE supervisor, or other Christian mental health professional.

As pastors, it is important for us to be in touch with our personal needs and to obtain professional help when we feel that we have lifestyle issues that seem to be beyond our ability to manage. We need to take good care of ourselves and to seek help for our personal needs rather than necessitate the intervention of others.

Conclusion

Let there be joy in the parish! God gives joy to His people as a special gift of His love. This joy is the joy of salvation, the joy of being His church, and the joy that comes from carrying out His purposes for His Church.

God wills that we and all His people find joy in worshiping Him around Word and Sacrament. God wants us to find joy in ministering to one another and to the world. For our ministry He equips us with Spirit-endowed functions and gifts to carry out our mission.

God, who calls people to be church and gives them a mission to carry forward, provides pastors for the care of His people. These pastors are to nurture God's people, to equip them for their Christian mission, and to join them in being Christ's presence in the lives of people of the world.

To carry out their ministry God gives authority to pastors to do Word and Sacrament ministry. This means that the pastor's authority is the authority of God's Word and the authority of serving according to that Word. Pastors are to serve in ways that make it possible for God's Gospel power to work in the lives of persons of every kind so that His purposes for His people are accomplished.

Since pastors represent Christ among the people, God bids His people to respect, obey, and provide for their spiritual leaders. He wants us to submit to their spiritual authority so that we receive rich benefits from their service. God has joined pastors and people together to share the joy of His plan for His people.

Unfortunately, there is often a lack of joy in the parish. Pastors and people alike exhibit a lack of correct understandings about God's plan for His people and behave in ways that diminish the joy that God wants His people to have. For example, pastors sometimes seek to control people for their personal advantage and sometime fail to equip others for service. Pastors also sometimes focus on looking correct rather than modeling the Christian life for those under their care.

Like pastors, people of the parish sometimes express wrong understandings and behaviors that diminish joy. They sometimes fail to pursue the togetherness that generates joy and fail rightly to regard the pastor.

Wrong understandings and behaviors on the part of both pastors and people destroy faithfulness and joy. They produce harmful competitiveness, personal and interpersonal hurt, and unfaithfulness in carrying forward the purposes of God.

Scripture, as we have observed, gives us clear statements about God's will for His church, the life together of pastors and people. In turn, contemporary writers give us assistance that I find consistent with biblical thought. They aid us in identifying and correcting our failures in carrying out God's will and assist us in facilitating God's plan.

From spokespeople of family systems theory we learn the importance for pastors and people of the concepts of self-differentiation, nonanxious presence, functional balance in systems, focus on process more than content in people relationships, overfunctioning, emotional triangles, and symptom bearer. The field of addictions informs us about the nature and hazards of codependency.

From our application of scriptural teachings and from Bible-compatible aspects of family systems and codependency concepts we learn how to become more competent, by God's forgiveness and life-renewing power, in carrying out God's purposes for our lives as pastors and people. In this pursuit we increasingly possess joy in our personal lives and in the parish.

How is joy in the parish possible? It is possible because of the forgiveness and life-transforming power that God makes available to us through His gift of faith in the saving life, death, and resurrection of Jesus Christ. It is only because of who Jesus is and what He has done for us to restore us to God's presence and power that we are given joy by God Himself. It is the splendid joy of our salvation, the joy of living in the fellowship of God's people, and the joy of carrying out God's purposes for His people. May God's power work mightily in our lives that we may honor Him and enjoy a full measure of His gift of joy. Let there be joy in the parish!

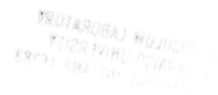

Works Cited

Clinebell, Howard J. *Understanding and Counseling Persons with Alcohol, Drug, and Behavioral Addictions*, rev. and enl. ed. Nashville: Abingdon Press, 1998.

"Clergy Shortage Study." Internet Address: http://higher-ed.lcms.org/pdf/clergy-shortage-study.pdf

Friedman, Edwin H. *Generation to Generation: Family Process in Church and Synagogue*. New York: the Guilford Press, 1985.

Knippel, Charles T. *The Twelve Steps: The Church's Challenge and Opportunity*. St. Louis: Concordia Publishing House, 1999.

_____. *When Addictions Threaten*. St. Louis: Concordia Publishing House, 2000.

Steinke, Peter L. *How Your Church Family Works*. Bethesda, MD: Alban Institute, Inc., 1993.

Tappert, Theodore, ed. and trans. *The Book of Concord*. Philadelphia: Fortress Press, 1959.

Wegscheider-Cruse, Sharon. *Another Chance: Hope and Health for the Alcoholic Family*, 2d ed. Palo Alto: Science and Behavior Books, Inc., 1989.